The Floral Year in Cross Stitch

Kaï and Denis Chabault
Ollivier Civiol

SEARCH PRESS

First published in Great Britain 2000

Search Press Limited
Wellwood, North Farm Road,
Tunbridge Wells, Kent TN2 3DR

Originally published in France 1999 by
Buchet/Chastel, Pierre Zech Éditeur, Paris
Original title: *Les fleurs des 4 saisons*
Copyright © Buchet/Chastel, Pierre Zech Éditeur, Paris 1999

Photography: Studio Delbord

English translation by Norman Porter
English translation copyright © Search Press Limited 2000

ISBN 0 85532 949 1

Contents

Getting started   4

Spring   8

Camellia   10
Clematis   11
Primrose   12
Narcissus   13
Tulip   14
Peony   15
Magnolia   16
Violet   17
Lily of the Valley   18
Daffodil   19
Iris   20
Peony   22
Spring Alphabet   23

Summer   24

Sunflower   26
Convolvulus   27
Lotus   28
Nasturtium   29
Lavender   30
Dog Rose   31
Rose   32
Campanula   33
Lotus   34
Poppy   35
Water Lily   36
Rose   38
Begonia   40
Summer Alphabet   41

Autumn   42

Morning Glory   44
Mirabilis   45
Nicotiana   46
Aster   47
Rudbeckia   48
Cyclamen   49
Montbretia   50
Anemone   51
Mallow   52
Hibiscus   53
Cup with Roses   54
Autumn Alphabet   56

Winter   58

Winter Aconite   60
Pansies   61
Christmas Rose   62
Crocus   63
Snowdrop   64
Mauve Pansy   65
Holly   66
Liverwort   67
Hellebore   68
Chionodoxa   69
Pansies   70
Winter Alphabet   72

Charts   73

Colour keys for the fold-out charts   117
DMC colour charts   126
Fold-out charts   Back sleeve

Getting started

To complete the designs successfully, it is recommended that you refer to the instructions below.

Choosing fabric

In order to make regular stitches, it is best to use fabric specially designed for cross stitch. The easiest material for beginners to work with is 'Aida'. This is made up of groups of warp and weft threads (usually four threads per group) which create a pattern of chequered squares, where they criss-cross each other. The stitch is embroidered on the squares.

Other fabrics can be used, such as linen, where the warp and weft threads criss-cross individually. Stitches are embroidered on two threads, horizontally and vertically. Because of its natural character, linen will give a warmer, more rustic appearance to your work.

Preparing the fabric

When you cut fabric to size, always leave a wide margin of approximately 10 cm (4in) all round the edge of the design. To prevent the edges from fraying, oversew them by hand, or machine-hem them.

To find the centre of the fabric, fold it into quarters, then mark a cross where the two folds intersect using a pencil or several tacking stitches.

For the more complex designs, start in one corner, just marking this corner and work in colour blocks from dark to light.

Threads

DMC stranded cotton no. 25 is used throughout this book. This consists of six separable strands, is available in skeins, 8m (26ft) long and it can be cut into equal lengths of 50cm (20in) maximum. To start, separate two of the six strands of one of these lengths and thread them together through the eye of a needle.

To combine two colours, take one strand of each colour and thread them together through the needle.

Needles

Cross stitch is embroidered with a tapestry needle. This has a blunt, rounded tip and an eye which is large enough to accommodate several strands of cotton. When working on linen with two strands, it is recommended that you use a no. 22 needle.

Charts

Charts are used in cross stitch embroidery. Here, specific symbols correspond to each cotton colour. Please note that the symbols are unique to each chart and are not transferable. Each square of the grid marked by a symbol corresponds to an individual cross stitch and all the unmarked squares indicate the fabric background.

To begin

When using small charts, it is easier to start stitching in the centre of the design. This is indicated on the chart by four arrows (see *Preparing the fabric* on page 4 for instructions on how to find the centre of the fabric).

For more complex designs, it is easier to start the embroidery in one of the corners and to work in colour blocks, beginning with the darkest colour and finishing with the lightest, so as to soil the work as little as possible.

Working cross stitches

Each little cross is made up of two stitches: the basic stitch below and the covering stitch on top. Make sure that the basic stitches are always worked from the bottom left to the top right, and the covering stitches from the bottom right to the top left.

To start a thread-length, secure the tail on the reverse side of the fabric with the first linking stitches. To finish off, pass the needle beneath several linking stitches on the reverse. Do not make any knots because they will form lumps which will remain visible.

Cross stitch can be worked in horizontal, vertical or diagonal lines. Work a series of basic stitches along the line and then work back, making the covering stitches in such a way as to form the cross stitches.

Never move to another block of the same colour, with the same thread, if it is more than 1.5 cm (½in) away. Instead, finish off, cut off the excess thread, then move to the next block and start again with a new length. When moving from one block to another if the distance is less than 1.5cm (½in), slip the thread beneath stitches that have already been worked.

With most of the more complex designs, you will have to thread different coloured strands through the needle at the same time.

Finishing off

When the work is finished it must be washed in cold water using a gentle shampoo, without rubbing the surface.

Rinse it in clear water, taking care not to wring or twist the surface of the material, then lay it flat to dry on a piece of clean linen. This will absorb any excess water.

Iron the embroidery before it is completely dry, placing a piece of clean linen over the area to be ironed.

Spring

9

Camellia

Chart on page 74

FLOWER	NO. OF COLOURS	NO. OF STITCHES	SIZE (CM)
Camellia	9	68 x 60	11.5 x 10

Chart on page 75

Clematis

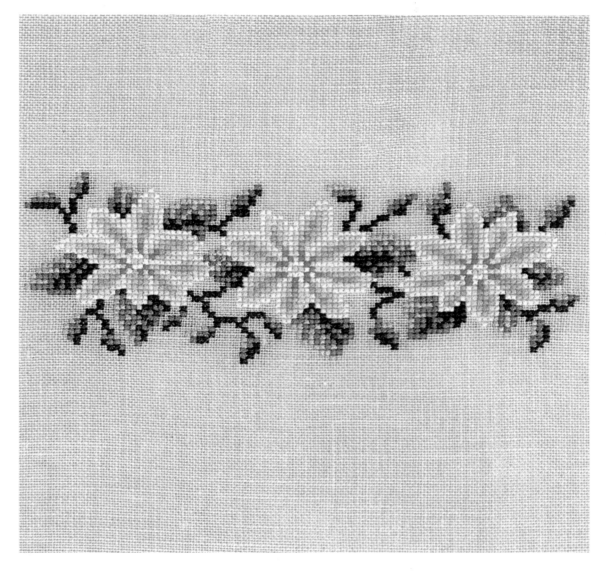

FLOWER	NO. OF COLOURS	NO. OF STITCHES	SIZE (CM)
Clematis	10	99 x 39	17.5 x 6

Primrose

Chart on page 76

FLOWER	NO. OF COLOURS	NO. OF STITCHES	SIZE (CM)
Primrose	12	69 x 93	12 x 15.5

Chart on page 77

Narcissus

FLOWER	NO. OF COLOURS	NO. OF STITCHES	SIZE (CM)
Narcissus	15	66 x 90	11.5 x 15

Tulip

Chart on page 78

FLOWER	NO. OF COLOURS	NO. OF STITCHES	SIZE (CM)
Tulip	19	65 x 96	11 x 16

Chart on page 79

Peony

FLOWER	NO. OF COLOURS	NO. OF STITCHES	SIZE (CM)
Peony	13	63 x 71	11 x 11.5

Magnolia

Chart on page 80

FLOWER	NO. OF COLOURS	NO. OF STITCHES	SIZE (CM)
Magnolia	13	69 x 58	11.5 x 9.5

Chart on page 81

Violet

FLOWER	NO. OF COLOURS	NO. OF STITCHES	SIZE (CM)
Violet	14	71 x 67	12 x 11

Lily of the Valley

Chart on page 82

FLOWER	NO. OF COLOURS	NO. OF STITCHES	SIZE (CM)
Lily of the valley	6	66 x 73	11.5 x 12

Chart on page 83

Daffodil

FLOWER	NO. OF COLOURS	NO. OF STITCHES	SIZE (CM)
Daffodil	13	63 x 82	10.5 x 13.5

Iris

Chart on pages 114–115

FLOWER	NO. OF COLOURS	NO. OF STITCHES	SIZE (CM)
Iris	58	88 x 77	15.5 x 14

Peony

Fold-out chart. Colour key on page 122

FLOWER	NO. OF COLOURS	NO. OF STITCHES	SIZE (CM)
Peony	58	165 x 165	30 x 30

Fold-out chart ## Spring Alphabet

NO. OF COLOURS	NO. OF STITCHES	SIZE (CM)
13	126 x 154	21 x 25

Summer

Sunflower

Chart on page 84

FLOWER	NO. OF COLOURS	NO. OF STITCHES	SIZE (CM)
Sunflower	11	58 x 80	10 x 13.5

Chart on page 85

Convolvulus

FLOWER	NO. OF COLOURS	NO. OF STITCHES	SIZE (CM)
Convolvulus	10	85 x 50	15 x 8

Lotus

Chart on page 86

FLOWER	NO. OF COLOURS	NO. OF STITCHES	SIZE (CM)
Lotus	11	40 x 50	6.5 x 7.5

Chart on page 87

Nasturtium

FLOWER	NO. OF COLOURS	NO. OF STITCHES	SIZE (CM)
Nasturtium	10	80 x 90	13.5 x 15.5

Lavender Chart on page 88

FLOWER	NO. OF COLOURS	NO. OF STITCHES	SIZE (CM)
Lavender	6	50 x 100	7.5 x 17.5

Chart on page 89

Dog Rose

FLOWER	NO. OF COLOURS	NO. OF STITCHES	SIZE (CM)
Dog rose	17	60 x 70	10.5 x 12

Rose

Chart on page 90

FLOWER	NO. OF COLOURS	NO. OF STITCHES	SIZE (CM)
Rose	10	50 x 60	8.5 x 10.5

Chart on page 91

Campanula

FLOWER	NO. OF COLOURS	NO. OF STITCHES	SIZE (CM)
Campanula	12	50 x 70	8.5 x 12

Lotus

Chart on page 92

FLOWER	NO. OF COLOURS	NO. OF STITCHES	SIZE (CM)
Lotus	13	40 x 70	6 x 11.5

Chart on page 93

Poppy

FLOWER	NO. OF COLOURS	NO. OF STITCHES	SIZE (CM)
Poppy	9	50 x 60	8.5 x 10

Water Lily

Fold-out chart

Colour key on page 120

FLOWER	NO. OF COLOURS	NO. OF STITCHES	SIZE (CM)
Water lily	120	122 x 117	23.5 x 22.5

Rose

Fold-out chart
Colour key on page 121

FLOWER	NO. OF COLOURS	NO. OF STITCHES	SIZE (CM)
Rose	100	112 x 110	19.5 x 19

Begonia

Fold-out chart
Colour key on page 123

FLOWER	NO. OF COLOURS	NO. OF STITCHES	SIZE (CM)
Begonia	107	143 x 209	30.5 x 43

Fold-out chart Summer Alphabet

NO. OF COLOURS	NO. OF STITCHES	SIZE (CM)
6	145 x 165	21.5 x 30

Autumn

utomne

43

Morning Glory Chart on page 94

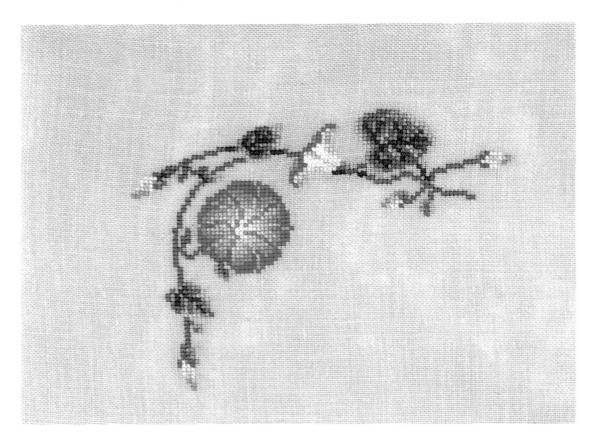

FLOWER	NO. OF COLOURS	NO. OF STITCHES	SIZE (CM)
Morning glory	18	92 x 74	16 x 11.5

Chart on page 95

Mirabilis

FLOWER	NO. OF COLOURS	NO. OF STITCHES	SIZE (CM)
Mirabilis	12	56 x 45	9.5 x 7

Nicotiana

Chart on page 96

FLOWER	NO. OF COLOURS	NO. OF STITCHES	SIZE (CM)
Nicotiana	20	45 x 59	7.5 x 9.5

Chart on page 97

Aster

FLOWER	NO. OF COLOURS	NO. OF STITCHES	SIZE (CM)
Aster	12	63 x 65	11 x 10.5

Rudbeckia

Chart on page 98

FLOWER	NO. OF COLOURS	NO. OF STITCHES	SIZE (CM)
Rudbeckia	11	57 x 86	10 x 14

Chart on page 99

Cyclamen

FLOWER	NO. OF COLOURS	NO. OF STITCHES	SIZE (CM)
Cyclamen	17	56 x 73	10 x 12

Montbretia

Chart on page 100

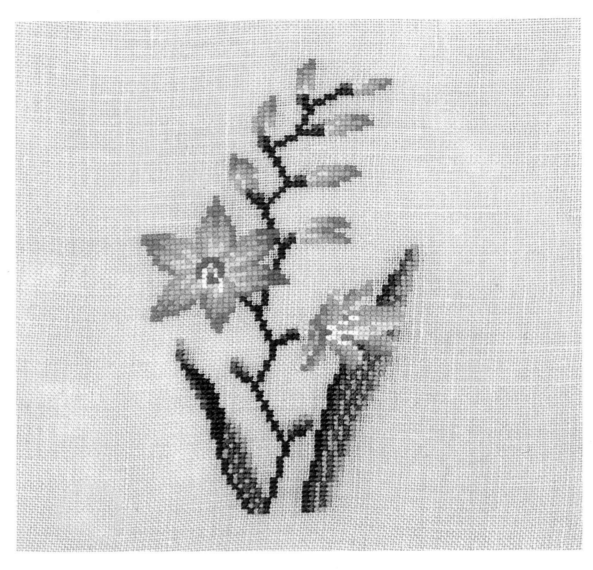

FLOWER	NO. OF COLOURS	NO. OF STITCHES	SIZE (CM)
Montbretia	10	52 x 91	9 x 15

Chart on page 101

Anemone

FLOWER	NO. OF COLOURS	NO. OF STITCHES	SIZE (CM)
Anemone	15	48 x 81	8 x 13.5

Mallow

Chart on page 102

FLOWER	NO. OF COLOURS	NO. OF STITCHES	SIZE (CM)
Mallow	10	64 x 80	11 x 13

Chart on page 103

Hibiscus

FLOWER	NO. OF COLOURS	NO. OF STITCHES	SIZE (CM)
Hibiscus	15	71 x 79	12 x 12.5

Cup with Roses

Fold-out chart

Colour key on pages 118-119

FLOWER	NO. OF COLOURS	NO. OF STITCHES	SIZE (CM)
Cup with roses	225	200 x 150	33.5 x 25.5

Autumn Alphabet

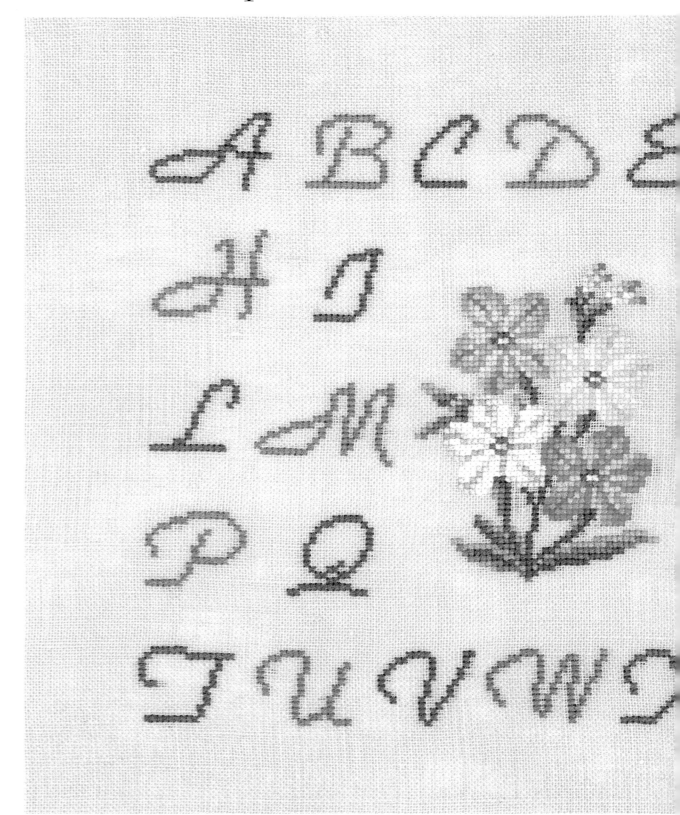

Fold-out chart

NO. OF COLOURS	NO. OF STITCHES	SIZE (CM)
20	140 x 116	23.5 x 22.5

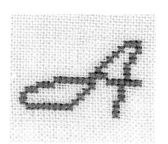

Winter

Winter Aconite

Chart on page 104

FLOWER	NO. OF COLOURS	NO. OF STITCHES	SIZE (CM)
Aconite	9	99 x 30	17 x 5

Chart on page 105

Pansies

FLOWER	NO. OF COLOURS	NO. OF STITCHES	SIZE (CM)
Pansies	23	100 x 36	16.5 x 6

Christmas Rose

Chart on page 106

FLOWER	NO. OF COLOURS	NO. OF STITCHES	SIZE (CM)
Christmas rose	15	85 x 87	14.5 x 15

Chart on page 107

Crocus

FLOWER	NO. OF COLOURS	NO. OF STITCHES	SIZE (CM)
Crocus	18	46 x 73	8 x 12

Snowdrop

Chart on page 108

FLOWER	NO. OF COLOURS	NO. OF STITCHES	SIZE (CM)
Snowdrop	9	58 x 80	9.5 x 14

Chart on page 109

Mauve Pansy

FLOWER	NO. OF COLOURS	NO. OF STITCHES	SIZE (CM)
Mauve pansy	13	55 x 70	9 x 12

Holly

Chart on page 110

FLOWER	NO. OF COLOURS	NO. OF STITCHES	SIZE (CM)
Holly	10	55 x 45	9 x 7.5

Chart on page 111

Liverwort

FLOWER	NO. OF COLOURS	NO. OF STITCHES	SIZE (CM)
Liverwort	15	78 x 85	13 x 14.5

Hellebore

Chart on page 112

FLOWER	NO. OF COLOURS	NO. OF STITCHES	SIZE (CM)
Hellebore	13	60 x 86	10 x 14

Chart on page 113

Chionodoxa

FLOWER	NO. OF COLOURS	NO. OF STITCHES	SIZE (CM)
Chionodoxa	11	53 x 96	8.5 x 16

Pansies

Fold-out chart. Colour
key on pages 124-125

NO. OF COLOURS	NO. OF STITCHES	SIZE (CM)
283	187 x 271	33 x 47

Winter Alphabet

NO. OF COLOURS	NO. OF STITCHES	SIZE (CM)
16	128 x 106	21.5 x 18.5

CHARTS

Camellia

68 x 60 stitches

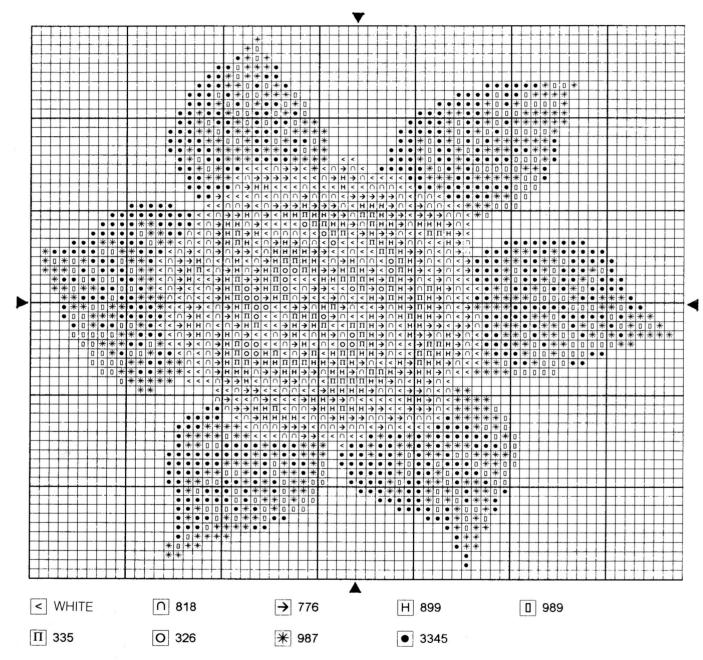

| < | WHITE | ∩ | 818 | → | 776 | H | 899 | ◻ | 989 |
| Π | 335 | O | 326 | ✳ | 987 | ● | 3345 |

Clematis

99 x 39 stitches

Symbol	Color		Symbol	Color
⧄	3348		♥	3345
X	899		✳	3347
↗	3716		=	309
T	3713		◻	335
v	745		N	3820

Primrose

69 x 93 stitches

`<` 772	`T` 727	`↑` 3824	`U` 894	`H` 725
`□` 722	`N` 893	`O` 471	`+` 335	`✳` 720
`●` 3347	`✔` 937			

Narcissus

66 x 90 stitches

Symbol	Color	Symbol	Color	Symbol	Color	Symbol	Color	Symbol	Color
<	WHITE	T	762	∩	369	→	415	U	973
H	3013	⧄	972	E	368	N	740	□	721
O	3012	+	606	✳	3011	●	367	♥	319

Tulip

65 x 96 stitches

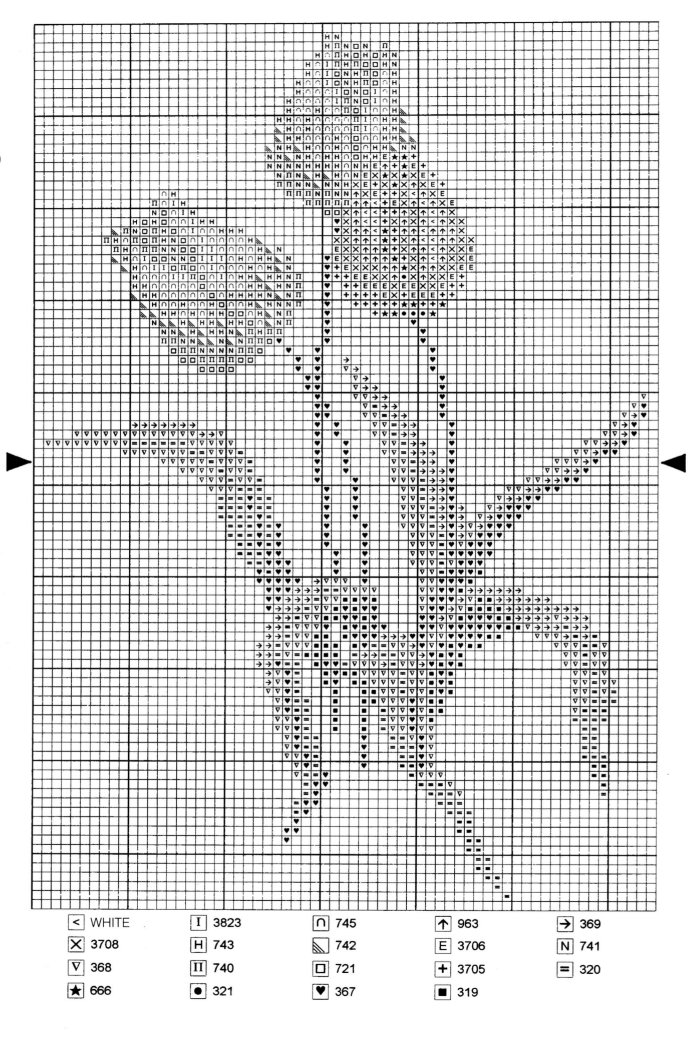

Symbol	Color	Symbol	Color	Symbol	Color	Symbol	Color	Symbol	Color
<	WHITE	I	3823	∩	745	↑	963	→	369
X	3708	H	743	◹	742	E	3706	N	741
V	368	Π	740	□	721	+	3705	=	320
★	666	●	321	♥	367	■	319		

Peony

63 x 71 stitches

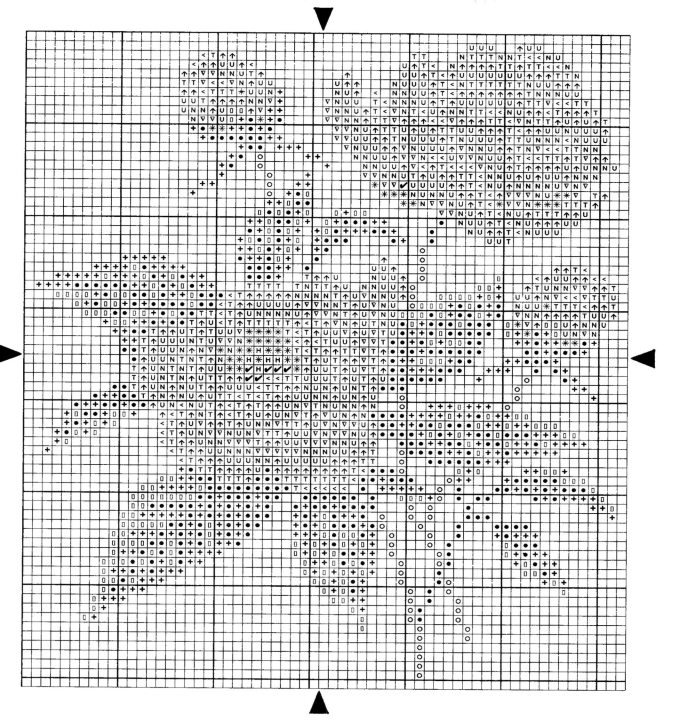

< WHITE	T 818	↑ 776	U 899	H 3820
▯ 989	N 335	∇ 309	O 580	+ 987
✳ 326	● 3345	✔ 498		

Magnolia

69 x 58 stitches

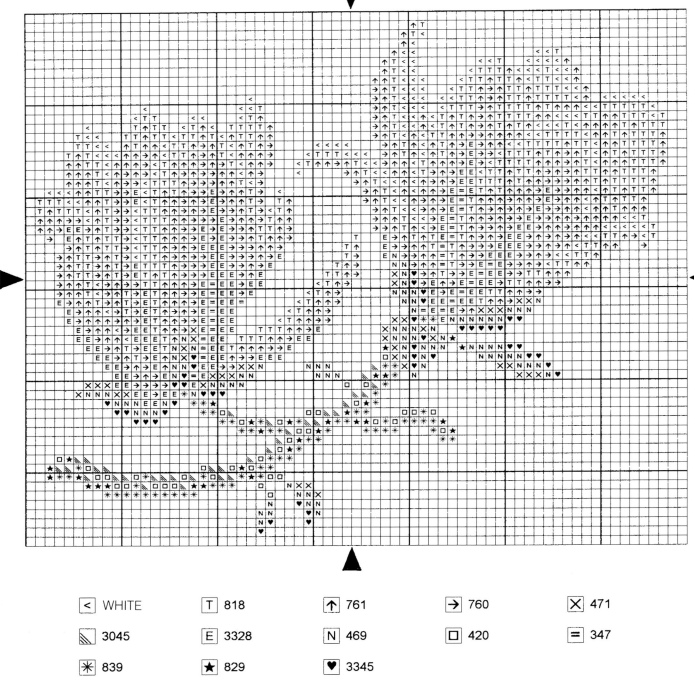

< WHITE	T 818	↑ 761	→ 760	✕ 471
◺ 3045	E 3328	N 469	☐ 420	= 347
✳ 839	★ 829	♥ 3345		

Violet

71 x 67 stitches

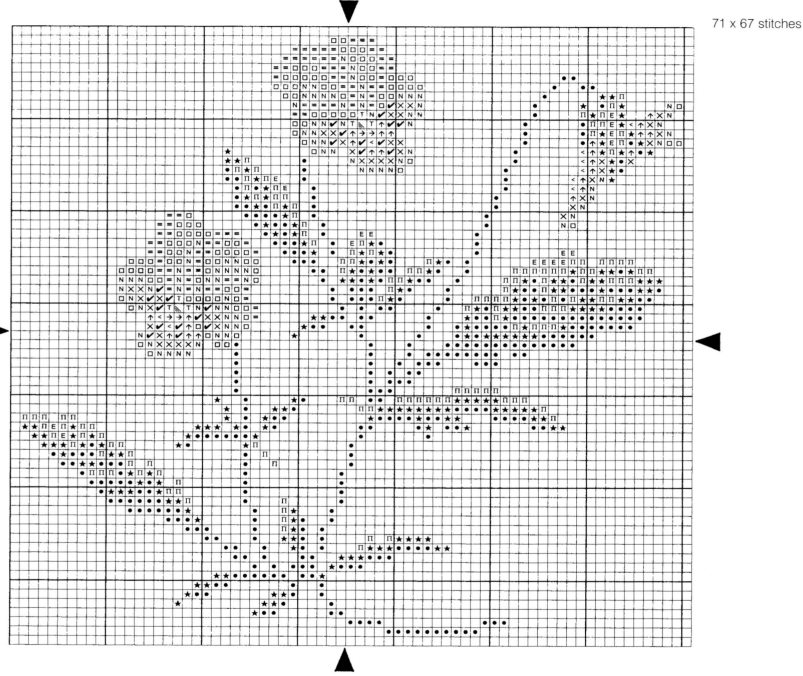

< WHITE	T 712	↑ 3747	→ 3078	X 341
◣ 973	E 3348	N 340	Π 471	□ 3746
= 333	★ 3346	● 520	✔ 310	

Lily of the Valley

66 x 73 stitches

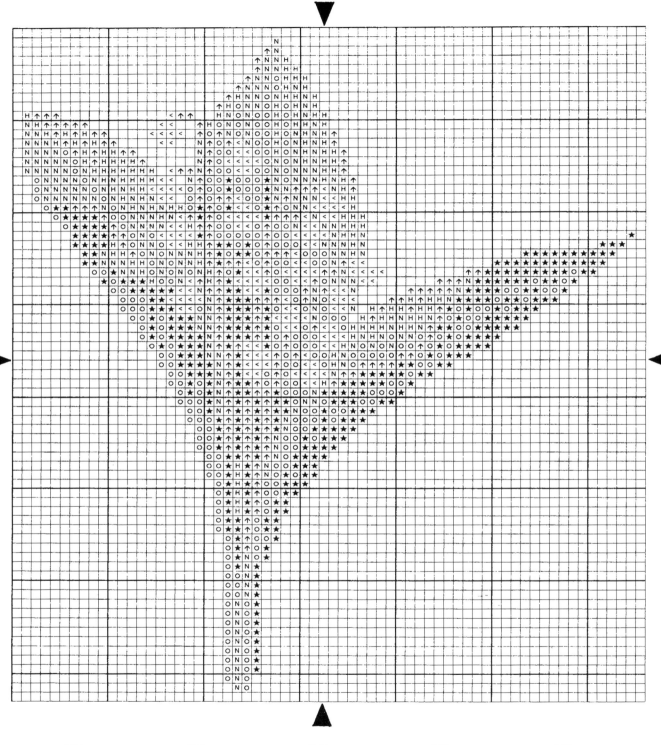

| < | WHITE | ↑ | 369 | H | 368 | N | 320 | O | 367 |

| ★ | 319 |

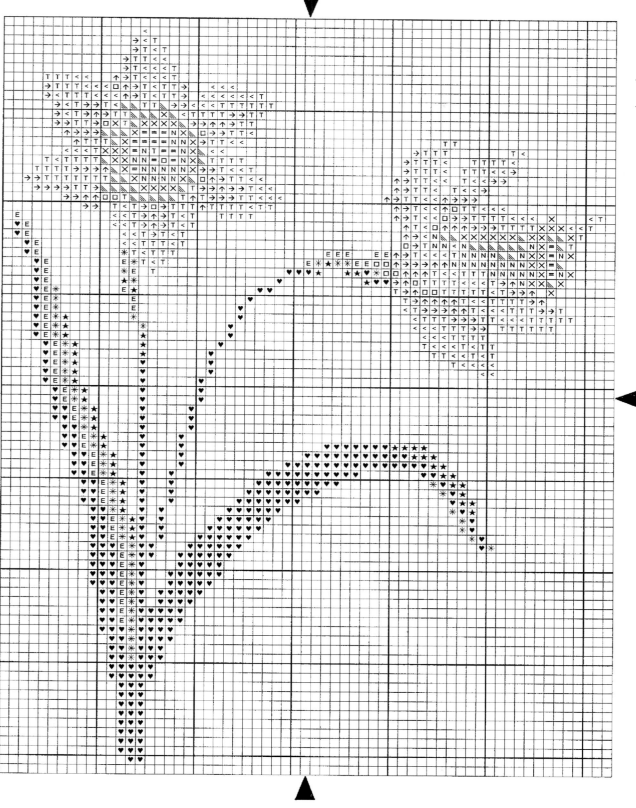

Daffodil

63 x 82 stitches

< 445	T 307	↑ 3820	→ 444	X 742
◸ 741	E 368	N 740	□ 783	= 720
✳ 320	★ 367	♥ 319		

Sunflower

58 x 80 stitches

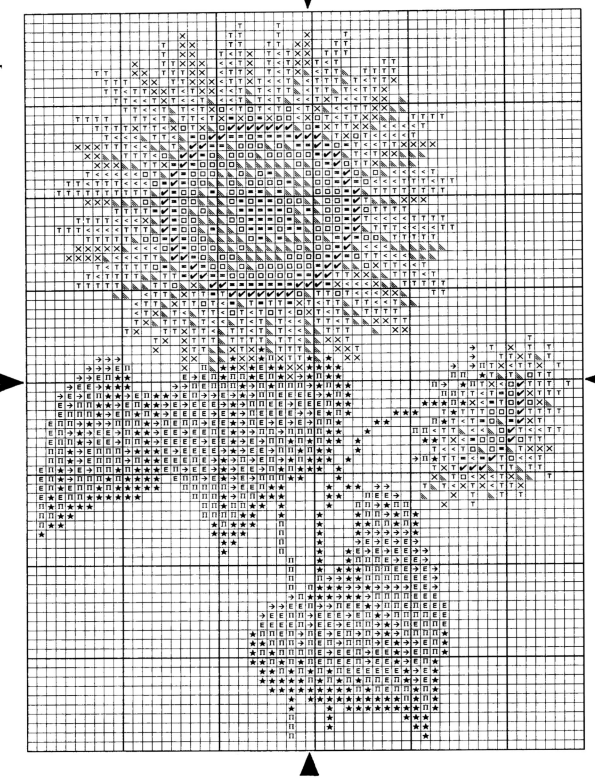

< 727	T 973	→ 3348	X 972	◣ 977
E 3347	Π 469	□ 3826	= 975	★ 3345
✔ 938				

Convolvulus

85 x 50 stitches

◹ 813	♥ 825		
☒ 827	✳ 987		
↑ 744	‖ 826		
T 3756	□ 989		
✓ WHITE	N 471		

Lotus

40 x 50 stitches

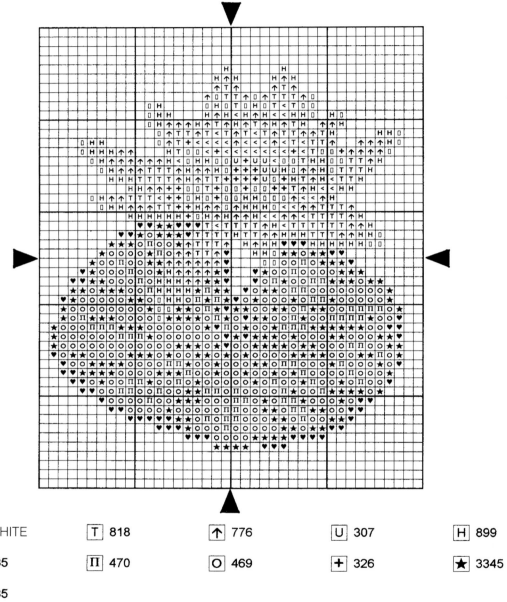

< WHITE	T 818	↑ 776	U 307	H 899
0 335	Π 470	O 469	+ 326	★ 3345
♥ 935				

Nasturtium

Opposite   80 x 90 stitches

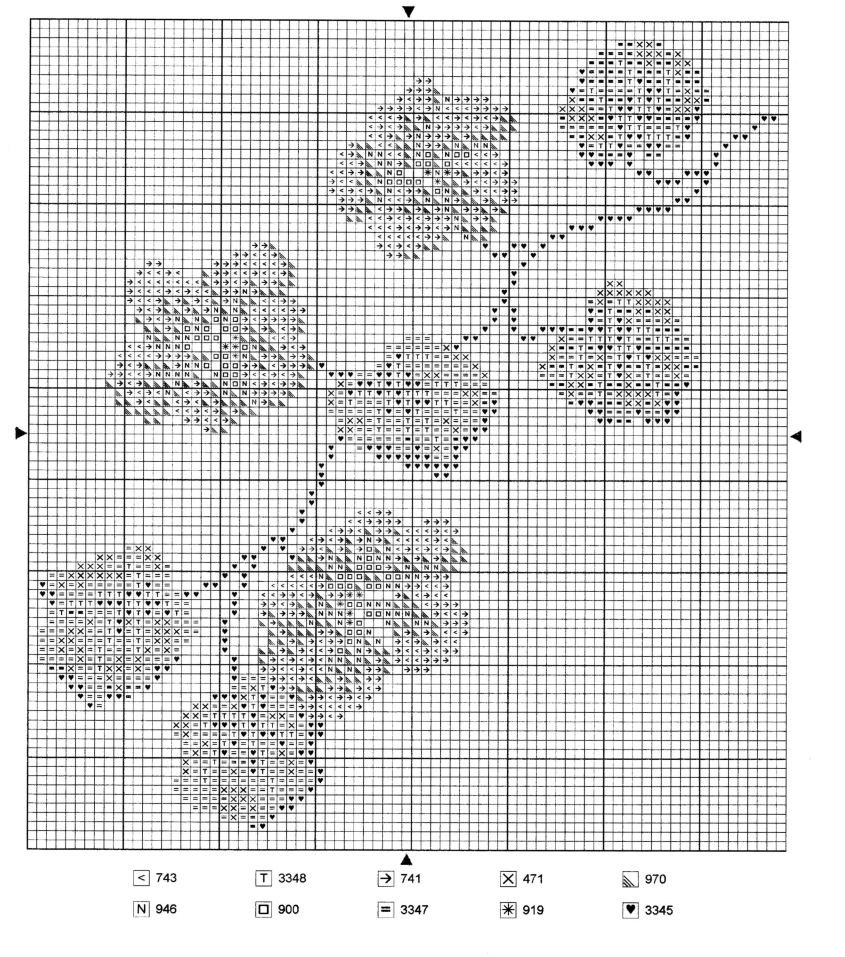

< 743	T 3348	→ 741	X 471	◣ 970
N 946	□ 900	= 3347	✳ 919	♥ 3345

Lavender

50 x 100 stitches

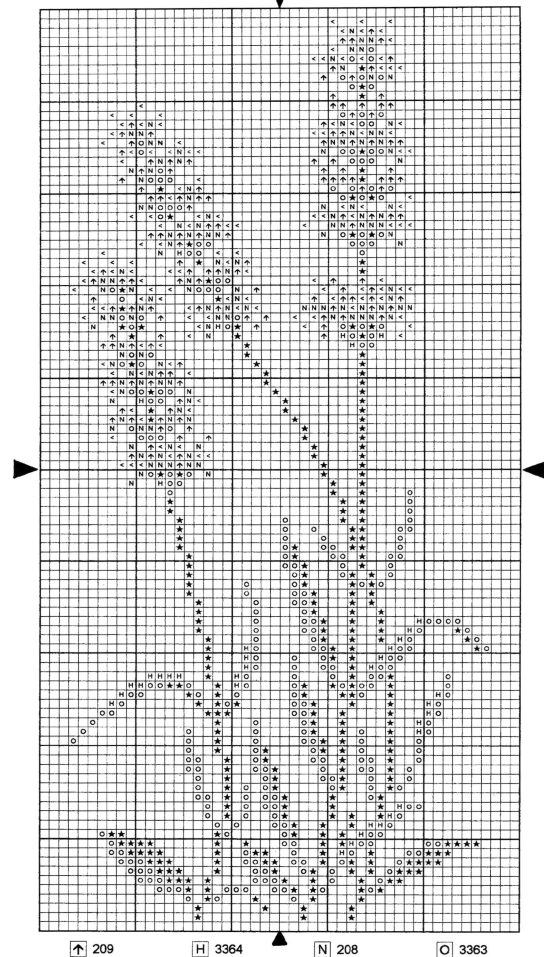

<< 211   ↑ 209   H 3364   N 208   O 3363   ★ 3362

Dog Rose

60 x 70 stitches

< 818	I 3770	∩ 745	↑ 963	→ 605
X 604	H 742	◺ 603	E 3364	N 602
□ 900	O 351	= 3363	✳ 3011	★ 350
● 830	■ 3362			

Rose

50 x 60 stitches

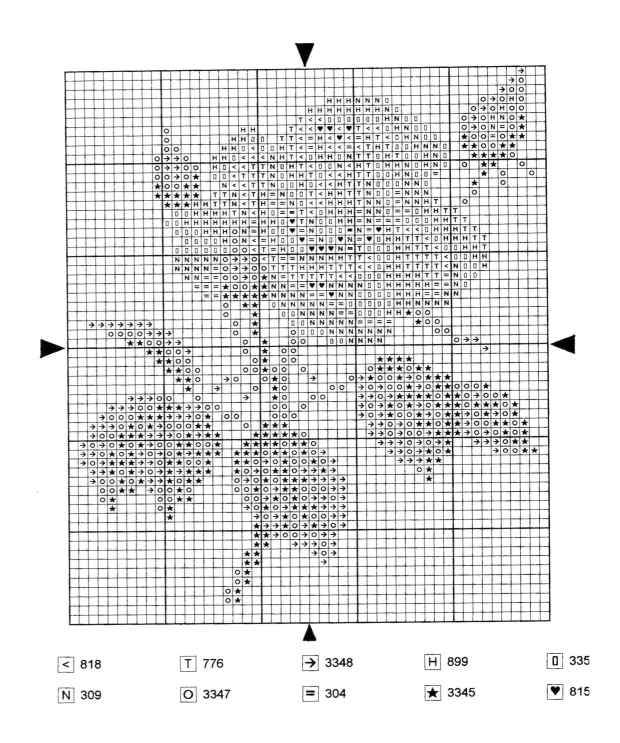

<	818	T	776	→	3348	H	899	◻	335
N	309	O	3347	=	304	★	3345	♥	815

Campanula

50 x 70 stitches

<	3326	T	341	↑	973	U	899	H	340
◻	335	N	783	Π	3746	O	309	+	3347
★	333	♥	3346						

Lotus

40 x 70 stitches

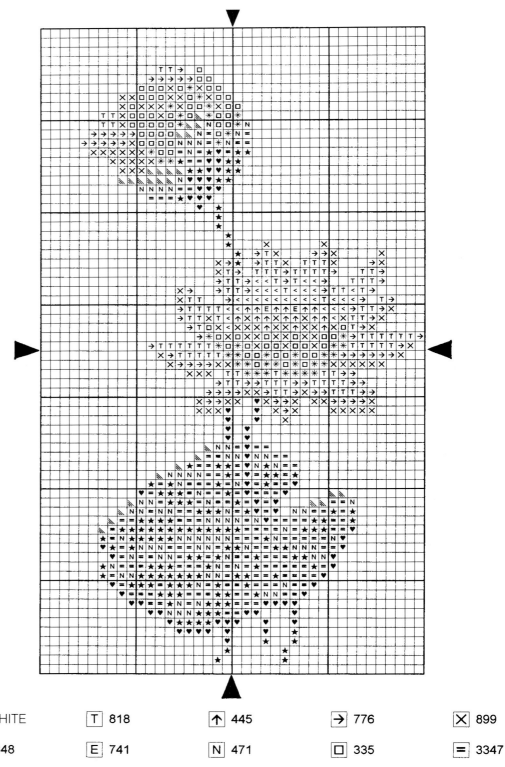

< WHITE	T 818	↑ 445	→ 776	X 899
◺ 3348	E 741	N 471	□ 335	= 3347
✳ 326	★ 3346	♥ 319		

Poppy

50 x 60 stitches

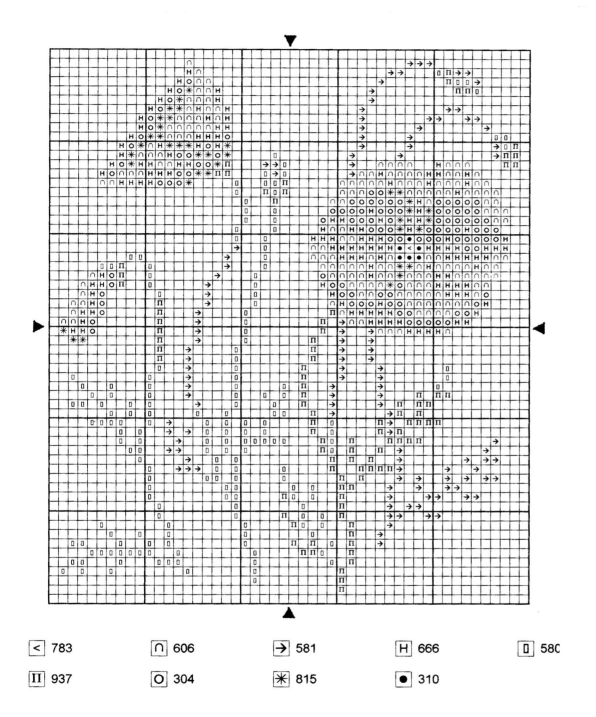

<	783	∩	606	→	581	H	666	▯ 580
Ⅱ	937	O	304	✳	815	●	310	

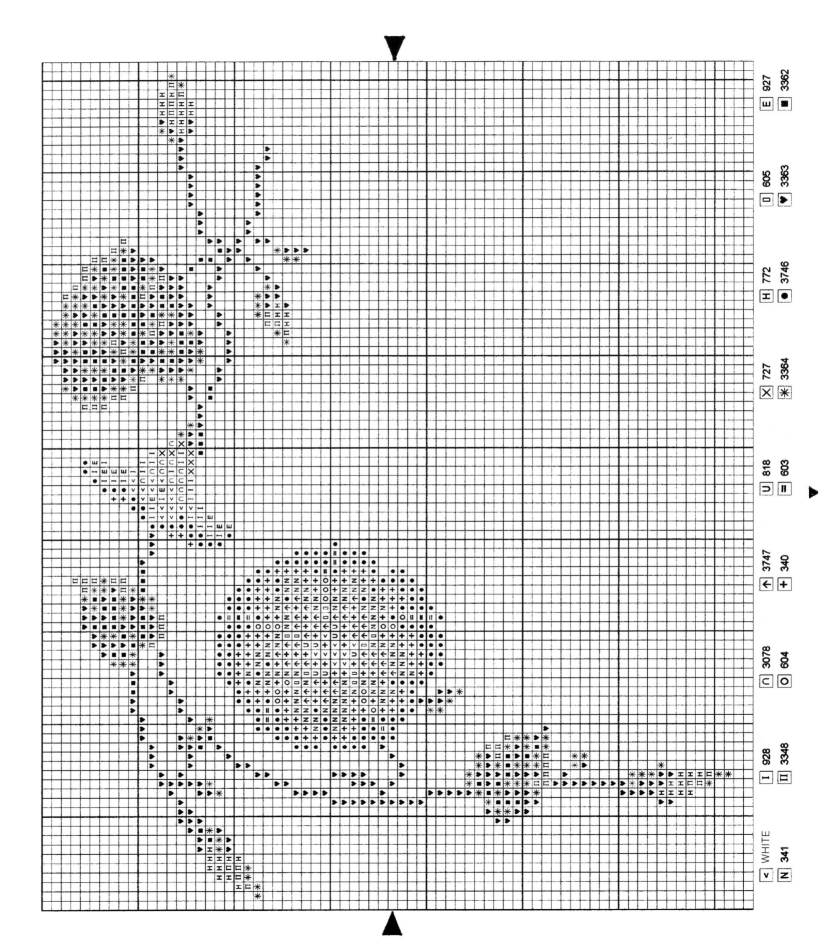

Mirabilis

56 x 45 stitches

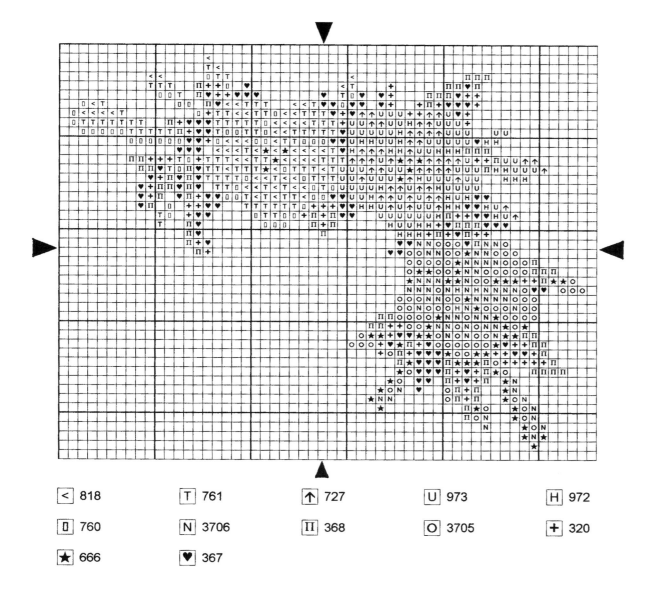

`<` 818	`T` 761	`↑` 727	`U` 973	`H` 972
`□` 760	`N` 3706	`Π` 368	`O` 3705	`+` 320
`★` 666	`♥` 367			

Morning Glory

Opposite   92 x 74 stitches

Nicotiana

45 x 59 stitches

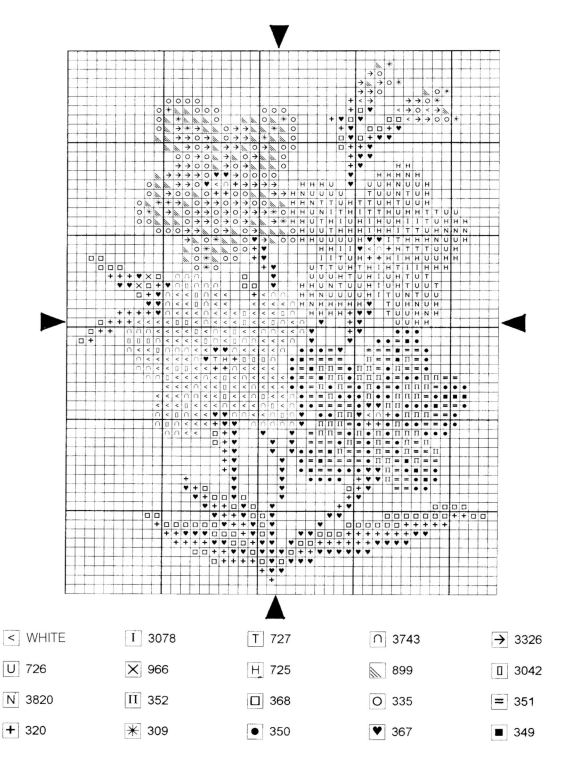

< WHITE	I 3078	T 727	∩ 3743	→ 3326
U 726	X 966	H 725	◣ 899	0 3042
N 3820	Π 352	□ 368	O 335	= 351
+ 320	✳ 309	● 350	♥ 367	■ 349

Aster

63 x 65 stitches

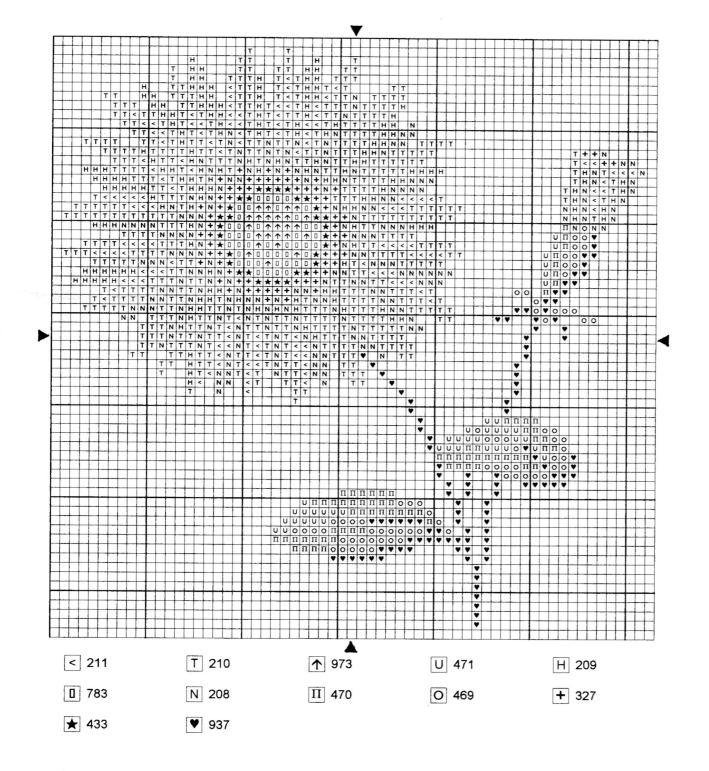

< 211	T 210	↑ 973	U 471	H 209
◫ 783	N 208	Ⅱ 470	O 469	+ 327
★ 433	♥ 937			

Rudbeckia

57 x 86 stitches

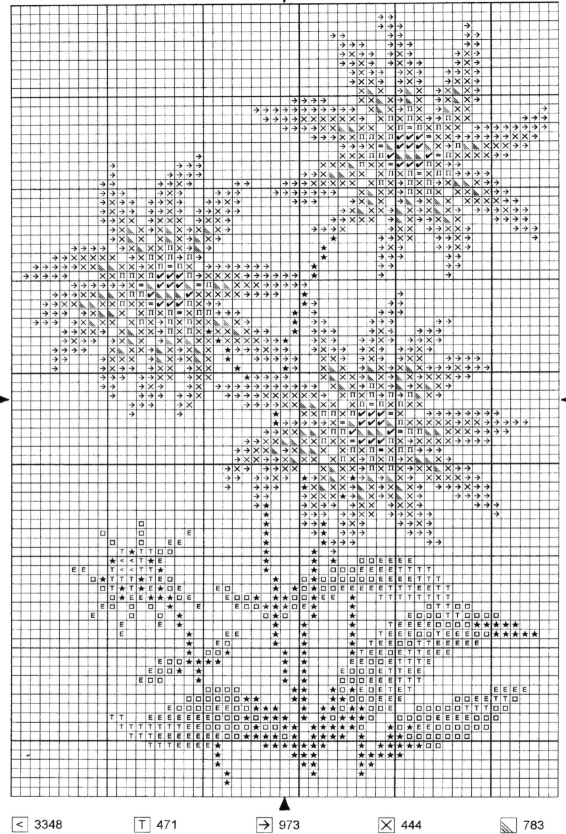

< 3348	T 471	→ 973	X 444	◩ 783
E 3347	Π 976	□ 3346	= 3826	★ 3345
✔ 975				

Cyclamen

56 x 73 stitches

`<` 818	`I` 605	`∩` 772	`↑` 604	`U` 3348
`X` 603	`◥` 602	`◻` 471	`N` 3045	`Π` 470
`◻` 601	`=` 420	`+` 600	`★` 3346	`●` 3051
`■` 869				

Montbretia

52 x 91 stitches

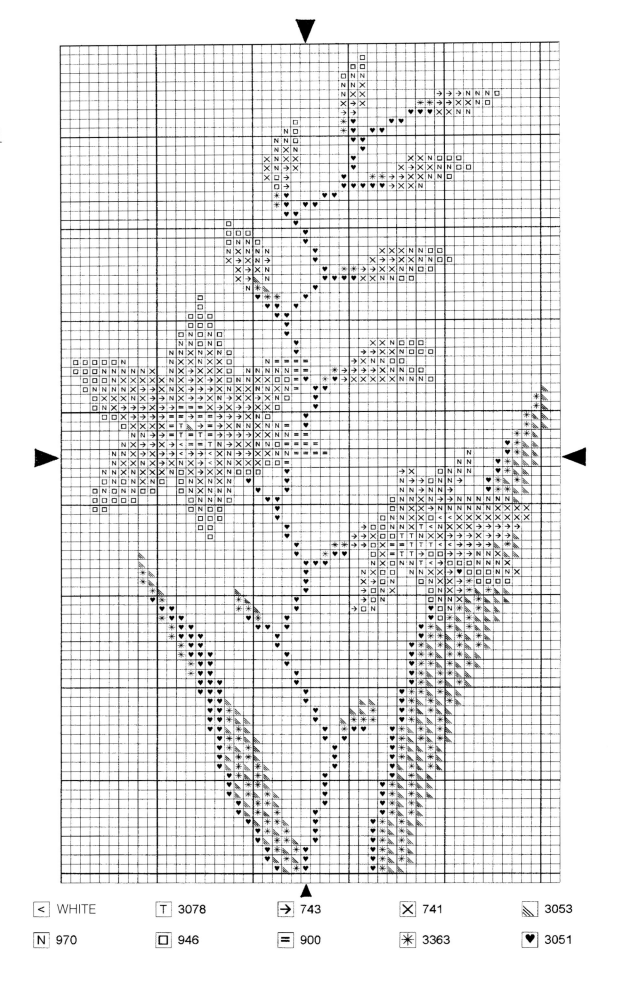

< WHITE	T 3078	→ 743	X 741	◣ 3053
N 970	□ 946	= 900	✳ 3363	♥ 3051

Anemone

48 x 81 stitches

< WHITE	T 951	∩ 727	→ 369	U 3779
H 842	◣ 368	E 3778	N 841	□ 581
O 320	+ 3830	✳ 580	● 869	♥ 367

101

Mallow

64 x 80 stitches

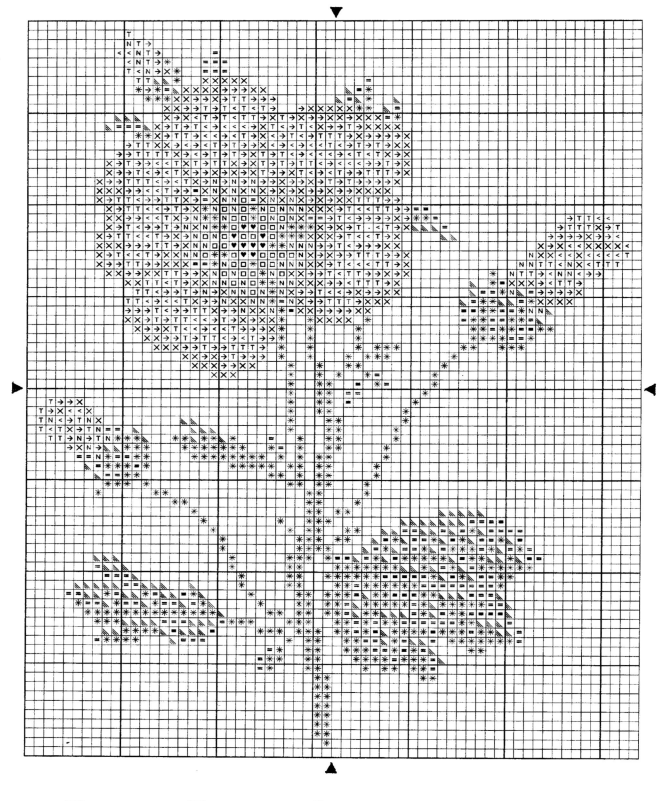

`<`	818	`T`	963	`→`	3716	`X`	962	`⧅` 471
`N`	961	`□`	3687	`=`	470	`✳`	937	`♥` 3803

Hibiscus

71 x 79 stitches

<	WHITE	T	543	∩	745	→	842	U	676
H	524	◩	3053	E	841	N	729	☐	3052
O	3328	+	3363	✳	304	●	3362	♥	310

Winter Aconite

99 x 30 stitches

<	3078	⊓	726
Π	471	O	581
→	3348	H	972
✳	3346	□	783
●	520		

Pansies

100 x 36 stitches

← 210	▨ 3820	∏ 208	✳ 3345	■ 898
∩ 445	H 972	v 3347	‖ 3346	↘ 823
T 3747	X 209	N 783	+ 350	◗ 550
I 211	U 307	E 340	□ 333	● 791
< WHITE	↑ 341	⊡ 444	O 3746	★ 815

105

Symbol	Color	Symbol	Color	Symbol	Color	Symbol	Color	Symbol	Color	Symbol	Color
<	WHITE	T	951	∩	727	→	369	U	842	H	973
◣	972	E	368	N	783	Π	841	☐	371	+	320
✳	370	★	367	♥	610	✔	319				

Crocus

46 x 73 stitches

Christmas Rose

Opposite   85 x 87 stitches

Symbol	Color	Symbol	Color	Symbol	Color	Symbol	Color	Symbol	Color	Symbol	Color
<	822	I	3747	∩	341	↑	743	U	3348	X	742
H	452	◻	613	E	741	N	340	Π	3041	O	3363
+	3746	=	841	✳	469	●	640	♥	327	■	935

107

Snowdrop

58 x 80 stitches

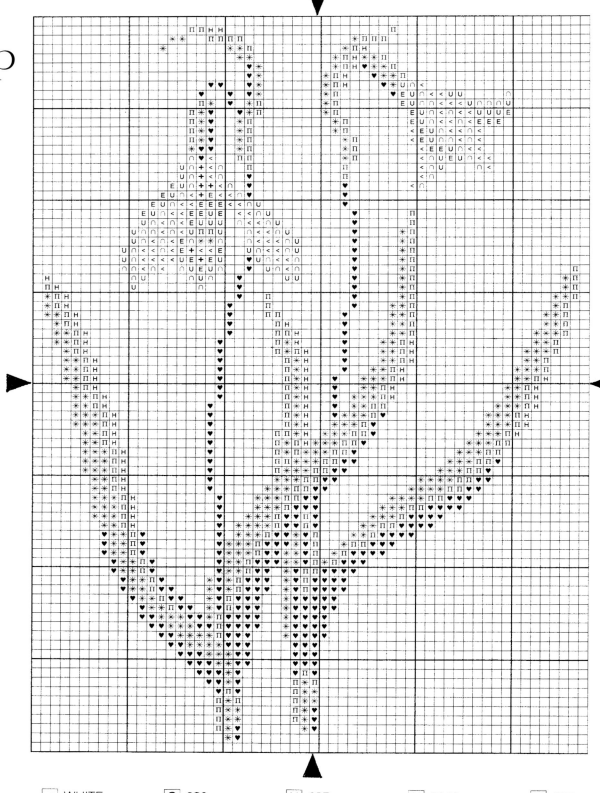

<	WHITE	∩	928	U	927	H	3348	E	926
II	471	+	3768	✳	3346	♥	520		

Mauve Pansy

55 x 70 stitches

Symbol	Color	Symbol	Color	Symbol	Color	Symbol	Color	Symbol	Color
<	WHITE	T	778	↑	3727	→	524	X	972
◣	316	E	3364	N	3726	□	900	=	3363
✳	3802	★	3362	♥	310				

Holly

55 x 45 stitches

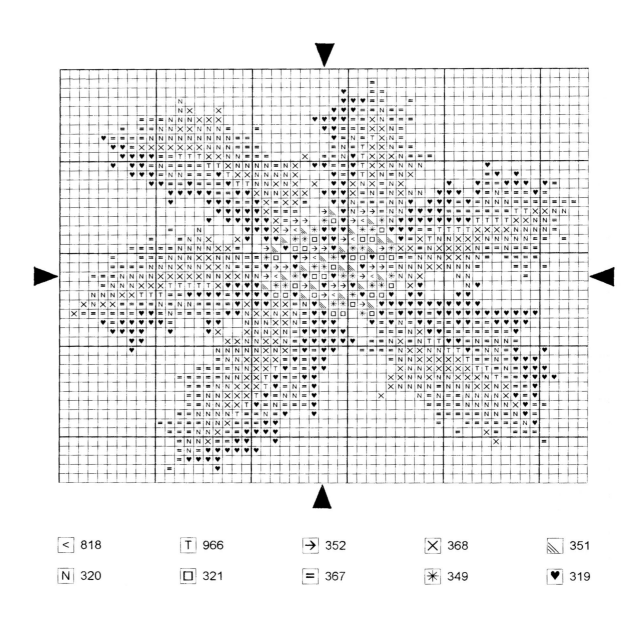

<	818	T	966	→	352	X	368	◹	351
N	320	□	321	=	367	✳	349	♥	319

Liverwort

Opposite   78 x 85 stitches

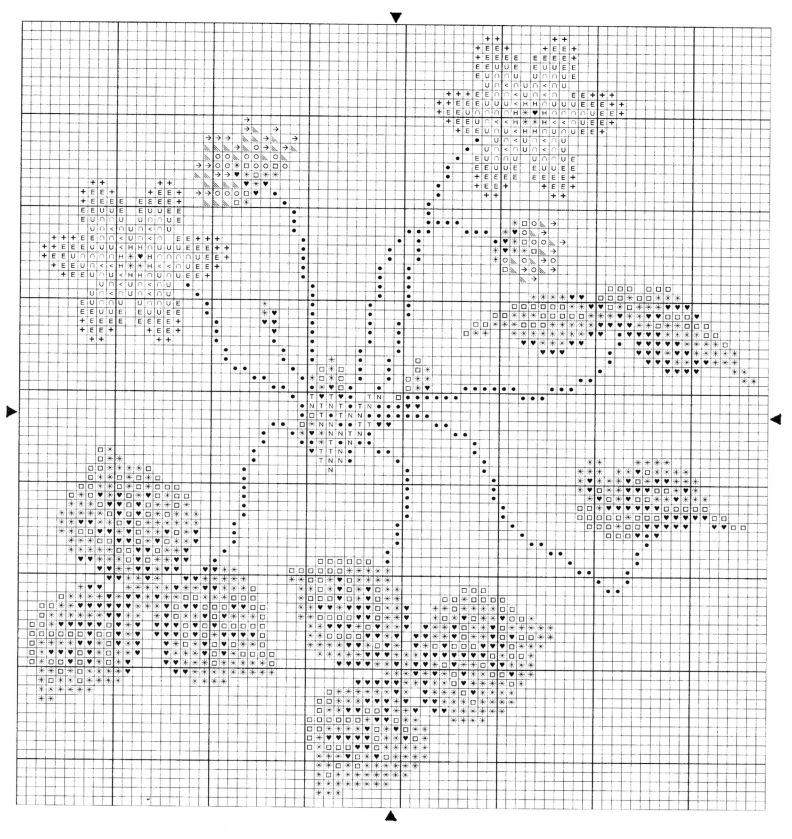

< WHITE	T 822	∩ 3747	→ 225	U 341
H 973	＼ 224	E 340	N 841	⬚ 3053
O 223	+ 3746	✳ 3052	● 611	♥ 3051

Hellebore

60 x 86 stitches

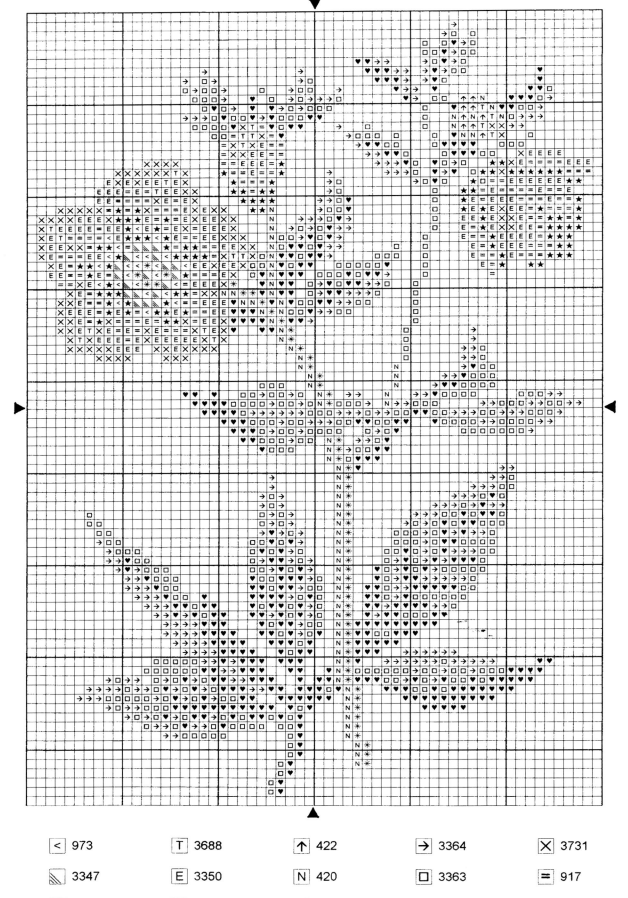

<	973	T	3688	↑	422	→	3364	X	3731
◢	3347	E	3350	N	420	□	3363	=	917
✳	869	★	327	♥	3362				

Chionodoxa

53 x 96 stitches

113

< WHITE	T 3689	↑ 727
0 3820	Π 3687	O 471
♥ 520		

U 3688	H 3348
+ 3803	★ 3346

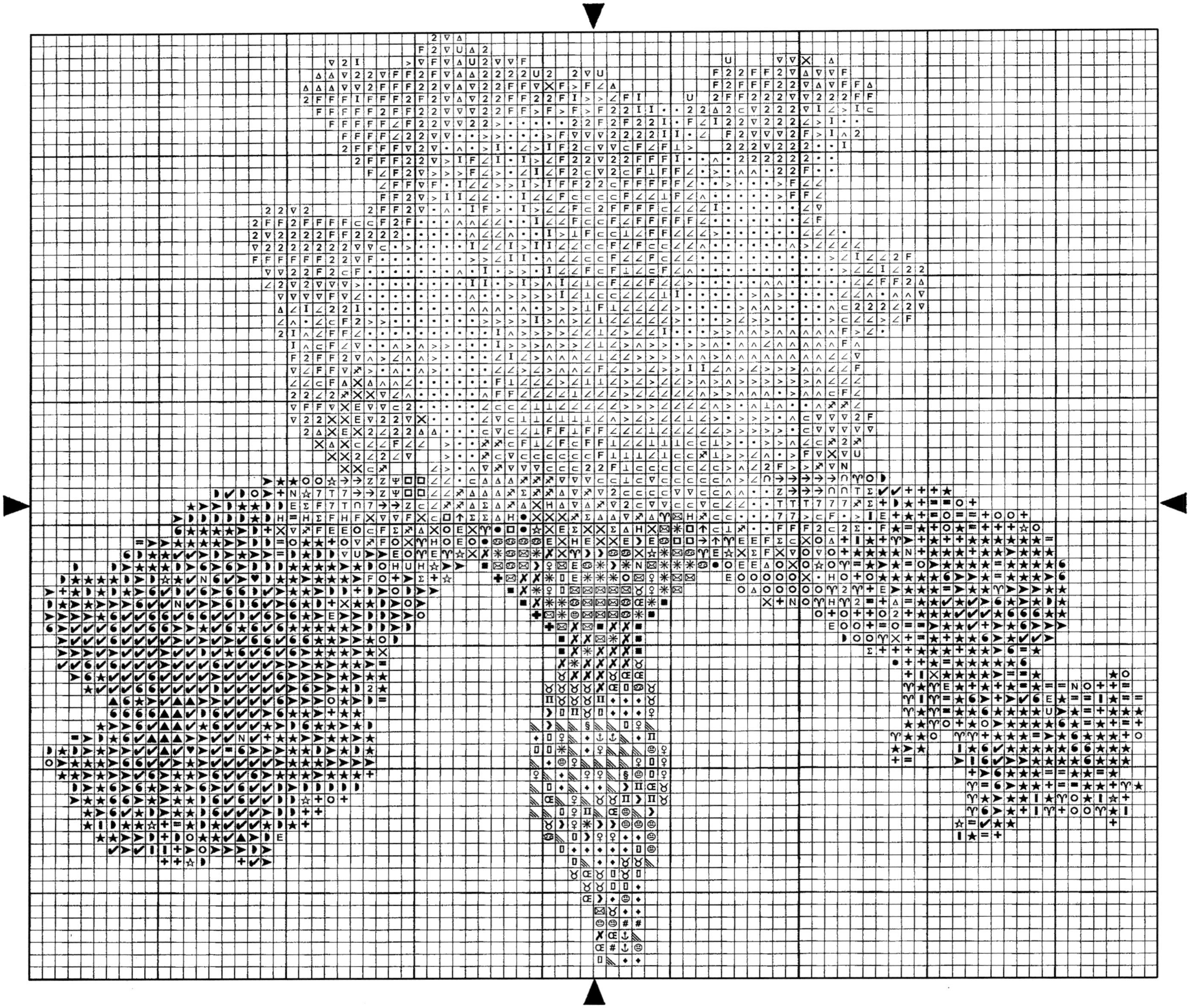

Iris

88 x 77 stitches

• WHITE	> WHITE +211	∧ WHITE +3747	7 3823	I WHITE +375
⊥ 211	∠ 211+3747	T 3823+744	F 211+3753	2 211+3752
⊂ 211+210	∩ 744	∇ 210+3752	↗ 210	→ 744+742
U 209+3752	Δ 210+209	↑ 554	Σ 209+554	◆ 524
X 209	Z 742	H 553+554	⧅ 524+522	⚓ 524+3364
E 553+209	Ψ 742+740	▯ 522+523	§ 522+3013	N 208+209
# 523+3364	Π 522+3364	♀ 3012+522	♉ 522	□ 721
O 552+209	❯ 3012	♈ 553	+ 208	Œ 522+3363
☆ 552+553	= 3746+208	☺ 3012+3363	♋ 3011+522	I 208+552
✳ 3012+3011	★ 333+208	● 552	◗ 3746+552	♥ 333+3746
➤ 333+552	✗ 3363+3011	⊠ 3011	☾ 333	✔ 327+333
■ 520+3011	▲ 327	✚ 3362		

115

COLOUR KEYS

FOR THE FOLD-OUT CHARTS

Cup
with
Roses

225 colours

Symbol	Code	Symbol	Code	Symbol	Code	Symbol	Code	Symbol	Code
∴	819+605	∧	762	∵	3689+819	…	818+776	»	963
«	3747	¿	762+3072	▲	819+3708	7	605	I	225+778
⊥	ECRU+453	▫	819+3354	7	762+453	≡	778	⊣	761
⊢	3743	T	3609+761	∠	3609	Ⴏ	762+415	}	3689
F	776	2	3689+3609	n	3072+453	3	3747+341	k	3326
√	963+894	Y	3716	)	604	f	224+762	⅃	3609+3708
⊂	453	+	225+224	h	415	∩	762+316	⊏	3743+3042
(	950	∇	3708	✗	3779	⁋	957	→	3824+3341
U	224+3824	△	604+603	↑	3713+3706	♦	453+224	⊃	3727
±	3354	⌣	761+760	{	3689+3688	⊂	3824+758	p	316+3072
b	894	d	3716+962	Σ	353+352	↙	3779+758	⌐	453+452
Þ	316+453	▷	224	ℵ	899	‡	3341	£	957+956
X	3689+3806	◁	894+758	6	603	9	3042	Z	950+3773
¤	316+3727	H	3733	μ	894+956	↵	758+224	Ɐ	894+893
½	758	▨	224+3688	◺	224+316	⊥	894+961	Ψ	962
E	894+3778	9	613+612	◗	956	m	452	D	3688
§	760	◀	316+452	▶	316	N	961+758	Λ	899+335
∈	316+3773	$	352	Ǝ	318	Ж	758+3778	⊟	3733+3731
¢	602+956	↦	956+961	#	760+3712	⌇	3041+3042	II	224+223
8	602	Ш	612	K	961	♀	402+3776	⇔	961+3778
þ	3687+3688	≋	316+3607	↕	3806	%	3778	æ	3712
W	3706+3705	♎	3731	O	891	□	335	Ƴ	452+451
❖	316+3726	¾	316+3772	⊋	602+3705	⌇	3778+356	⅋	3805
❯	316+317	Υ	351	&	3712+3328	⊼	3041	W	608+720
●	3687	♑	356	Æ	611+612	⌇	891+3801	∞	3705

Symbol	Colour	Symbol	Colour	Symbol	Colour	Symbol	Colour	Symbol	Colour
	355+3830		3772+632		355		350		839+840
	732+3362		731+730	?	469+937		3051		646
	919	@	3740		3721		632		919+918
★	3011+936		830	●	937		349		580+936
	400		610	♥	730		3721+221		400+610
	3362+3051		3787+3022		645+646		347		839
♠	829+830		520	X	221	✉	300+632		300+3777
	3362		300+400	✔	300+610	✱	935+730	■	645
♣	829		936	✳	535		3787		814+347
	300	▲	934+520		934+3362		935	✚	3781
☎	844+645	▼	934+935		814		934		3021
	3031+934		844	◆	3031		310+3685	X	535+310
	310+3021	■	310+844	●	310	·	819	\	WHITE +762
−	WHITE	:	WHITE +3756	/	WHITE +819	!	WHITE +3743	1	3713+819
Γ	818	>	WHITE +963	L	3747+3756		3772+355	S	3607+3772
	900	⊗	840		3705+3801	☆	223		356+3830
	3607+355	⊙	3772+317		3726	Œ	414	Ø	720
	920	¶	666+3801		921+920	=	3705+900		601
☺	3328		3801		611	+	921	⇒	3041+3740
	451		3772		317		351+350		3830

119

Water Lily

120 colours

•	WHITE	╲	819+818	/	WHITE +225	>	ECRU+948	⌐	WHITE +3689
⌐	3770+963	−	ECRU+3689	∧	WHITE +3609	▲	WHITE +3774	7	951
I	948	▫	712+3609	⊥	712+3774	T	822	Ч	948+3609
7	WHITE +725	≡	WHITE +742	⊣	3689+3609	├	739	╎	225+945
∠	677	2	3609	F	3609+3774	«	3689+604	⊐	945
+	3774+3033	∩	745+742	⊂	3609+604	⊏	604+3774	U	951+444
Λ	951+972	↑	677+676	∇	3047	↗	744+742	⊣	604
→	783+ECRU	Σ	950	⌒	3033+453	⌣	745+741	⬋	677+444
↖	3354	◆	676	⊂	842	)	3608	⫽	782+ECRU
╲	644	‡	453+224	X	676+444	◁	832+ECRU	▷	725+722
N	783+677	$	472+444	§	3727	⋇	758	⊟	972+742
μ	224+3013	Z	444	↦	224+437	H	437+3013	#	224+834
Ψ	725+740	𝕀	444+741	Π	782+677	⊍	402	⚓	224+3773
E	3688	⇔	224+3782	♀	3046+834	↕	444+971	O	3773+3013
୪	972+971	□	3782+3013	❖	422+834	❭	444+907	γ	783+444
♠	224+3045	%	733+3013	℔	3782	+	834+729	Œ	833+834
☆	3773+729	S	3782+729	=	3064	☺	972+720	Ø	782+444
&	3778	𝒳	722+921	⊙	972+921	β	3046+782	☒	832+444
▌	972+817	⇨	783	𝔔	407	✳	676+831	✚	733+3045
▦	740+720	➤	972+321	⬍	3773+832	★	444+831	⊠	907+782
●	782+783	𝔇	972+919	♥	832+783	✖	3045+782	▶	976
⌐	680	6	782	✉	740+919	X	907+831	♠	922+919
⦂	817	✔	781	■	782+831	▲	780	✚	919
▼	580+730	▌	400	◆	730	✖	829	●	898

Rose

100 colours

− WHITE	/ ECRU+818	\ WHITE +963	⌐ 819+963	└ 819+951
« 818+3713	∧ ECRU+3689	... 948	» 951	I 819+353
⊥ 963+3689	∠ 818+353	? 225	≡ 225+3689	⊦ 951+754
2 948+353	⊂ 605	+ 225+3779	∩ 3779+3689	(951+3341
Y 3713+3341	f 353	✗ 3779	3033	U 950
↑ 604	{ 353+3341	⌒ 3341+3779	Σ 3354	⬉ 453
♦ 842	◁ 778	£ 3024	א 3341	⋈ 3727
μ 224	∀ 758	◩ 352	▨ 3706	Ψ 722
∈ 603	§ 760	◀ 437	$ 402	E 3688
∃ 415	⊟ 3340	# 741	¢ 834	ᵟ 422
⌐ 648	⋋ 452	⇔ 977	þ 351	↕ 3782
□ 892	❖ 372	⌇ 318	¾ 316	⟩ 3064
W 3712	& 721	ℎ 922	⌢ 436	◗ 407
Œ 642	☆ 833	= 3731	☺ 733	℔ 946
er 3052	⊗ 3032	G 223	∽ 356	⊙ 647
⊙ 3776	▮ 976	? 680	⇨ 900	✳ 921
¶ 370	✚ 435	Æ 3722	★ 3011	⬍ 3022
) 832	♥ 611	‼ 920	➤ 355	◖ 321
X 420	✔ 3790	■ 919	♣ 830	☜ 400
☎ 730	▥ 829	▌ 300	◆ 814	■ 898

Peony

58 colours

▣ WHITE	▷ 819	∧ 3770	7 746	I 948
⊥ 822	∠ 963	T 761	F 945	2 754
⊂ 3326	∩ 3774	∇ 3743	↗ 353	→ 957
U 3825	△ 778	↑ 894	Σ 472	◆ 224
✕ 899	Z 524	H 722	◣ 613	⚓ 760
E 893	Ψ 523	▯ 224+3712	§ 3773	N 224+223
# 892	Π 961	♀ 522	♉ 3712	▫ 352
O 612	❯ 452	♈ 223+3712	✛ 223	Œ 470
☆ 3328	= 3722	☺ 3772	♋ 3363	▮ 309
✳ 3347	★ 642	● 580	◗ 3051	♥ 3721
▶ 3346	✗ 520	✉ 221	◖ 3362	✔ 935
■ 934	▲ 934+844	✚ 844		

Begonia

107 colours

Symbol	Colour	Symbol	Colour	Symbol	Colour	Symbol	Colour	Symbol	Colour
•	WHITE	\	WHITE +819	>	819	L	818+ WHITE	Γ	818+819
∧	818	I	819+963	▲	3713+818	7	963	⊥	3713
□	353+818	∠	963+3716	T	3326+963	Ч	761	7̄	353+3713
≡	776+3716	⊣	893+819	⊦	3716	2	3326+776	F	3326+3716
∩	3326	⊏	353	⊏	819+892	+	3706+3713	↗	3713+352
⁹	3716+894	→	818+892	U	3326+894	Δ	761+760	↑	894
∇	351+761	↙	3713+946	↖	352+894	◆	892+3326	Σ	3716+3705
⊂	3706	⌣	352	◲	3706+352	▨	893	◁	894+891
▷	894+3705	N	893+892	§	606+894	✳	3706+946	X	350+3706
⊟	352+946	Z	894+309	#	894+817	↦	892	H	352+606
E	321+894	Ψ	351+350	□	352+817	Π	891	Ш	3705+891
⚓	3705	♀	321+3706	⇔	946	↕	606+891	Ծ	3705+606
⊡	817+891	❖	891+309	O	892+326	⟩	3705+817	Υ	606
◖	606+309	☺	606+817	₧	907+904	+	817+309	Œ	309
☆	817	S	321+606	=	581+580	✗	907+909	⊙	321+817
ℬ	326	♋	321	I	581+909	✻	580	⇨	904+580
⚡	904	✚	321+498	▦	3777+498	≻	580+909	⊠	904+909
⬍	321+815	★	580+3345	●	498+815	◗	909	♥	580+895
✗	730	➤	3345+909	◗	815	◖	938+321	∿	895+909
✗	3345	♠	814+815	⚑	3345+895	✔	829	■	814
▲	895	✚	3371+815	▼	890+895	▮	310+814	◆	890
✖	890+310	●	310						

123

Pansies

283 colours

Symbol	Colour	Symbol	Colour	Symbol	Colour	Symbol	Colour	Symbol	Colour
−	WHITE	:	819+WHITE	/	3756+WHITE	•	3823+WHITE	\	3756
⌐	211+WHITE	>	WHITE+822	L	747+3756	⌐	3078+WHITE	1	747
∴	WHITE+955	∧	WHITE+772	∵	828+3756	…	WHITE+3753	»	3747+3756
«	746+3078	¿	504+WHITE	▲	WHITE+762	7	3753+3756	I	445+3823
⊥	3743+WHITE	⊡	211	7	ECRU+543	≡	211+3747	⊣	3747
⊦	3078	T	775+3325	∠	504+ECRU	4	928	}	445
F	ECRU+3072	2	369	n	772	3	369+772	]	955+772
k	3747+800	≤	928+504	)	727	∫	504+369	⌐	211+210
⊂	677	+	3747+341	h	762	∩	800	⊏	ECRU+3024
(	3753+3752	√	3743	λ	747+3766	z	445+307	Y	564+772
U	928+927	Δ	ECRU+453	↑	3325+3755	∇	822+644	↗	472+772
⌐	677+676	⌐	524+369	→	3348+772	C	524+772	p	3072
b	955+954	d	827	Σ	210	↙	800+809	⌐	341
Þ	3819+772	◆	966	⊃	543+842	±	564	⌣	794+3747
{	307	◁	834+772	6	927	9	554	▷	472
™	762+415	א	210+209	‡	809	£	369+368	X	3743+3042
⌣	3813+503	⌴	524	∞	794+800	Z	3348	⇓	307+444
⇑	954	⇐	209	⇒	644	∀	3752+932	½	809+799
H	341+340	⌐	3755+334	μ	444+3820	⌐	524+523	□	444
⧄	3819	⧅	966+368	⚓	503	Ψ	907+472	E	472+471
∈	3053+3348	$	3072+648	§	954+913	m	613	N	453
◀	972	▶	3013	Λ	799	D	3033+3782	⊔	554+553
⊇	415	⋇	523	Ω	563	Ǝ	989+3348	B	3042
↦	927+926	⊢	913	⌐	340	Π	3053	⌐	209+208
⊔	334	L	932	K	794	♀	907	⇔	368
≈	453+452	þ	613+612	#	316	¢	996	⊤	834+833
æ	3364+471	W	704+907	↕	993+992	%	503+502	❖	522
ø	471+470	⟩	704	Œ	208	⌐	3816+3815	⌐	334+322
¾	563+562	●	648	&	783	Ω	799+798	⌐	907+906

Pansies

283 colours

=	932+931	☺	703	+	3042+3041	ℓ	3052	K	553+552
↗	783+782		988	↘	833+832		793		322
er	906		318		502	✳	3746		798
U	581	⊗	992+3814	X	703+702	G	832		552
✈	926+3768	⊙	988+987		562	B	911	⇒	793+3807
⊞	906+905	¶	452+451	★	522+520		3746+333		702
	798+797	I	318+414		208+327	✳	831+832	u	470+469
↕	917	D	3726		905	⇨	3041		702+701
?	3768		3814		3347	✛	320+367	✳	333
+	731	➤	451		831	⊠	797	⬍	905+904
★	469	✳	987+986	H	701	●	3807+792		917+915
⁙	435+434		333+327	➝	3765		831+830	✳	904
⊖	3363+3362	@	501	♥	552+550	✂	367	☢	792
	700	➤	414+317		797+796		3346		3768+924
	937		327		434	♠	915		730
X	561	✉	991+924		333+791		930	—	610
	937+936		434+433	✔	986+319		796	♣	501+500
	730+935	■	792+791		327+791		646+645		924
✹	796+820		3345		3750		520+934	◄	550
(	535	▲	327+823		433+801	⊕	3362+934		820
	500		3781		791	✚	895+934	♠	935+934
☎	814	▼	3750+939		550+939		934	≡	898
	820+939	➡	890		791+939		939		3685+310
✳	924+310	◆	535+310	X	3799+310	P	500+310	L	814+310
S	934+310	■	890+310	●	939+310		415+318	Z	340+3746
	733	♉	704+471	□	3364		833		794+793
O	912+913	Υ	3053+3052	W	553		989	Æ	704+703
	3023		989+988	☆	368+320				

125

TABLEAU DE RECHERCHE DES COULEURS - KEY TO COLOUR NUMBERS
FARBTABELLE - TABEL OM KLEUREN UIT TE ZOEKEN - TABELLA RICERCA COLORI
TABLA PARA BUSCAR LOS COLORES - QUADRO DE PROCURA DAS CORES
FARVENUMMER OVERSIGT - FÄRGSÖKNINGSTABELL - TABELA KOLORÓW

颜色代号卡 - カラー番号表 - جدول تحديد الألوان

N°Couleur - Colour No - Farbnr. - Nr Kleur - N° colore - N° Color - N° Cor
Farve nr. - Färg nr. - Nr. koloru - 颜色代号 - カラー番号 - رقم اللون

Colonne - Column - Spalte - Kolom - Colonna - Columna - Coluna
Kolonne - Kolumn - Kolumna - 列 - 欄 - العمود

N°	Col	N°	Col	N°	Col	N°	Col	N°	Col	N°	Col	N°	Col	N°	Col	N°	Col	N°	Col
ECRUT	22	211	6	400	19	563	11	727	17	813	8	910	11	971	18	3347	12	3773	20
BLANC	22	221	5	402	19	564	11	729	16	814	2	911	11	972	18	3348	12	3774	20
B5200	22	223	5	407	20	580	14	730	14	815	2	912	11	973	18	3350	3	3776	19
48	24	224	5	413	23	581	14	731	14	816	2	913	11	975	19	3354	3	3777	20
51	26	225	5	414	23	597	9	732	14	817	1	915	4	976	19	3362	13	3778	20
52	24	300	19	415	23	598	9	733	14	818	3	917	4	977	19	3363	13	3779	20
53	26	301	19	420	16	600	4	734	14	819	3	918	19	986	12	3364	13	3781	22
57	24	304	2	422	16	601	4	738	21	820	7	919	19	987	12	3371	21	3782	22
61	26	307	17	433	21	602	4	739	21	822	22	920	19	988	12	3607	4	3787	22
62	24	309	3	434	21	603	4	740	17	823	8	921	19	989	12	3608	4	3790	22
67	25	310	23	435	21	604	4	741	17	824	8	922	19	991	10	3609	4	3799	23
69	26	311	8	436	21	605	4	742	17	825	8	924	10	992	10	3685	3	3801	2
75	24	312	8	437	21	606	18	743	17	826	8	926	10	993	10	3687	3	3802	5
90	26	315	5	444	17	608	18	744	17	827	8	927	10	995	9	3688	3	3803	3
91	25	316	5	445	17	610	15	745	17	828	8	928	10	996	9	3689	3	3804	4
92	25	317	23	451	23	611	15	746	16	829	15	930	7	3011	15	3705	2	3805	4
93	25	318	23	452	23	612	15	747	9	830	15	931	7	3012	15	3706	2	3806	4
94	26	319	12	453	23	613	15	754	1	831	15	932	7	3013	15	3708	2	3807	7
95	24	320	12	469	13	632	20	758	20	832	15	934	13	3021	22	3712	1	3808	9
99	24	321	2	470	13	640	22	760	1	833	15	935	13	3022	22	3713	1	3809	9
101	25	322	8	471	13	642	22	761	1	834	15	936	13	3023	22	3716	2	3810	9
102	24	326	3	472	13	644	22	762	23	838	21	937	13	3024	22	3721	5	3811	9
103	26	327	6	498	2	645	23	772	12	839	21	938	21	3031	22	3722	5	3812	10
104	26	333	6	500	11	646	23	775	8	840	21	939	8	3032	22	3726	5	3813	11
105	26	334	8	501	11	647	23	776	3	841	21	943	10	3033	22	3727	5	3814	10
106	26	335	3	502	11	648	23	778	5	842	21	945	20	3041	5	3731	3	3815	10
107	24	336	8	503	11	666	2	780	16	844	23	946	18	3042	5	3733	3	3816	10
108	26	340	6	504	11	676	16	781	16	869	16	947	18	3045	16	3740	5	3817	10
111	26	341	6	517	9	677	16	782	16	890	12	948	1	3046	16	3743	5	3818	11
112	24	347	1	518	9	680	16	783	16	891	1	950	20	3047	16	3746	6	3819	14
113	25	349	1	519	9	699	14	791	7	892	1	951	20	3051	13	3747	6	3820	17
114	25	350	1	520	13	700	14	792	7	893	1	954	11	3052	13	3750	7	3821	17
115	24	351	1	522	13	701	14	793	7	894	1	955	11	3053	13	3752	7	3822	17
116	24	352	1	523	13	702	14	794	7	895	12	956	2	3064	20	3753	7	3823	17
121	25	353	1	524	13	703	14	796	7	898	23	957	2	3072	23	3755	8	3824	18
122	25	355	20	535	23	704	14	797	7	899	3	958	10	3078	17	3756	8	3825	18
123	25	356	20	543	21	712	21	798	7	900	18	959	10	3325	8	3760	9	3826	19
124	25	367	12	550	6	718	4	799	7	902	5	961	2	3326	3	3761	9	3827	19
125	25	368	12	552	6	720	18	800	7	904	14	962	2	3328	1	3765	9	3828	16
126	24	369	12	553	6	721	18	801	21	905	14	963	2	3340	18	3766	9	3829	16
208	6	370	15	554	6	722	18	806	9	906	14	964	10	3341	18	3768	10	3830	20
209	6	371	15	561	11	725	17	807	9	907	14	966	12	3345	12	3770	20		
210	6	372	15	562	11	726	17	809	7	909	11	970	18	3346	12	3772	20		

EMBROIDERY THREADS DMC

Stranded Cotton, D. 117 - Pearl Cotton Art. 115 No. 3 ● No. 5 ○ - Pearl Cotton Art. 116 No. 5 ▲ No. 8 △ No. 12 ▽

1
3713, 761, 760, 3712, 3328, 347, 948, 754, 353, 352, 351, 350, 349, 817, 894, 893, 892, 891

2
963, 3716, 962, 961, 957, 956, 3708, 3706, 3705, 3801, 666, 321, 304, 498, 816, 815, 814

3
819, 818, 776, 3326, 899, 335, 309, 326, 3354, 3733, 3731, 3350, 3689, 3688, 3687, 3803, 3685

4
3806, 3805, 3804, 605, 604, 603, 602, 601, 600, 3609, 3608, 3607, 718, 917, 915

5
225, 224, 223, 3722, 3721, 221, 778, 3727, 316, 3726, 315, 3802, 902, 3743, 3042, 3041, 3740

6
554, 553, 552, 550, 211, 210, 209, 208, 327, 3747, 341, 340, 3746, 333

7
794, 793, 3807, 792, 791, 800, 809, 799, 798, 797, 796, 820, 3753, 3752, 932, 931, 930, 3750

8
3756, 775, 3325, 3755, 334, 322, 312, 311, 336, 823, 939, 828, 827, 813, 826, 825, 824

9
3761, 519, 518, 3760, 517, 996, 995, 747, 3766, 807, 806, 3765, 3811, 598, 597, 3810, 3809, 3808

10
964, 959, 958, 3812, 943, 993, 992, 3814, 991, 928, 927, 926, 3768, 924, 3817, 3816, 3815

11
504, 3813, 503, 502, 501, 500, 564, 563, 562, 561, 955, 954, 913, 912, 911, 910, 909, 3818

12
966, 369, 368, 320, 367, 319, 890, 989, 988, 987, 986, 772, 3348, 3347, 3346, 3345, 895

13
524, 523, 522, 520, 3053, 3052, 3051, 3364, 3363, 3362, 472, 471, 470, 469, 937, 936, 935, 934

14
704, 703, 702, 701, 700, 699, 907, 906, 905, 904, 3819, 581, 580, 734, 733, 732, 731, 730

15
3013, 3012, 3011, 372, 371, 370, 834, 833, 832, 831, 830, 829, 613, 612, 611, 610

16
3047, 3046, 3045, 422, 3828, 420, 869, 783, 782, 781, 780, 746, 677, 676, 729, 680, 3829

17
3822, 3821, 3820, 445, 307, 444, 3078, 727, 726, 725, 3823, 745, 744, 743, 742, 741, 740

18
973, 972, 971, 970, 947, 946, 900, 608, 606, 3824, 3341, 3340, 3825, 722, 721, 720

19
922, 921, 920, 919, 918, 402, 3776, 301, 400, 300, 3827, 977, 976, 3826, 975

20
3770, 951, 945, 3774, 950, 3773, 3064, 407, 3772, 632, 3779, 758, 3778, 356, 3830, 355, 3777

21
712, 739, 738, 437, 436, 435, 434, 433, 801, 898, 938, 3371, 543, 842, 841, 840, 839, 838

22
B5200, BLANC, ECRUT, 3024, 3023, 3022, 3021, 822, 644, 642, 640, 3790, 3033, 3782, 3032, 3781, 3031

23
453, 452, 451, 535, 3072, 648, 647, 646, 645, 844, 762, 415, 318, 414, 317, 413, 3799, 310

24
48, 116, 62, 112, 107, 57, 75, 115, 99, 95, 126, 52, 102

25
124, 93, 113, 121, 103, 67, 91, 123, 125, 101, 114, 122, 92

26
94, 104, 90, 108, 51, 106, 111, 61, 105, 69, 53